discovermore

Learning Social Studies Skills

Exploring Artifacts

Marie Harts

Britannica Educational Publishing

IN ASSOCIATION WITH

THE ROSEN PUBLISHING GROUP

Published in 2025 by The Rosen Publishing Group, Inc.
2544 Clinton Street, Buffalo, NY 14224

Editor: Shannon Harts
Book Design: Michael Flynn

Photo Credits: Cover, p. 25 Sun_Shine/Shutterstock.com; (series background) Dai Yim/Shutterstock.com; p. 4 https://commons.wikimedia.org/wiki/File:Bronze_Mirror_from_Satellite_Tomb_(9907995994).jpg; p. 5 Viacheslav Lopatin/Shutterstock.com; p. 6 Jaclyn Vernace/Shutterstock.com; p. 7 https://commons.wikimedia.org/wiki/File:Pectoral_and_Necklace_of_Sithathoryunet_with_the_Name_of_Senwosret_II_MET_DT531.jpg; p. 8 thipjang/Shutterstock.com; p. 9 Hasmat18/Shutterstock.com; p. 11 (top) ImAAm/Shutterstock.com; p. 11 Bukhta Yurii/Shutterstock.com; p. 13 (top) lego 19861111/Shutterstock.com; p. 13 (bottom) Andre Silva Pinto/Shutterstock.com; p. 14 Harmony Gerber/Shutterstock.com; p. 15 a katz/Shutterstock.com; p. 16 Baloncici/Shutterstock.com; p. 17 luisrsphoto/Shutterstock.com; p. 18 https://commons.wikimedia.org/wiki/File:Willard_Libby_in_Lab.jpg; p. 19 Clare Louise Jackson/Shutterstock.com; p. 20 Anton Chalakov/Shutterstock.com; p. 21 Mariana_Rusanovschi/Shutterstock.com; p. 22 Wangkun Jia/Shutterstock.com; p. 23 https://commons.wikimedia.org/wiki/File:The_inspection_team_sets_up_the_ground-penetrating_radar_equipment_(15709616830).jpg; p. 24 JurateBuiviene/Shutterstock.com; p. 26 Daniel J. Rao/Shutterstock.com; p. 27 Fabian Leu/Shutterstock.com; p. 28 Mistervlad/Shutterstock.com; p. 29 Jaclyn Vernace/Shutterstock.com.

Library of Congress Cataloging-in-Publication Data

Names: Harts, Marie, author.
Title: Exploring artifacts / Marie Harts.
Description: [Buffalo] : Britannica Educational Publishing, [2025] | Series: Discover more! Learning social studies skills | Includes bibliographical references and index.
Identifiers: LCCN 2023051578 | ISBN 9781641901413 (library binding) | ISBN 9781641901406 (paperback) | ISBN 9781641901420 (ebook)
Subjects: LCSH: Antiquities--Juvenile literature. | Archaeology--Juvenile literature. | Excavations (Archaeology)--Juvenile literature.
Classification: LCC CC171 .H38 2025 | DDC 930.1--dc23/eng/20231214
LC record available at https://lccn.loc.gov/2023051578

Manufactured in the United States of America

CPSIA Compliance Information: Batch #CSBRIT25. For further information contact Rosen Publishing at 1-800-237-9932.

Contents

An Underground Discovery

In September 2023, Israel officials announced that a team of archaeologists had uncovered a 2,300-year-old tomb on a rocky slope along a highway. Inside the tomb were the remains of a Greek woman, and clues about who she was. These clues included a bronze folding mirror. The archaeologists believed this mirror would have been expensive when the woman was alive. This means it could have been given to her as a gift before a wedding. This led the archaeologists to think perhaps the woman was traveling in Israel with a high-ranking member of the Greek army.

Bronze mirrors are examples of artifacts that people used in their daily lives. Many artifacts can be found in museums, such as this bronze mirror that was placed in the Qianling Museum in Shaanxi Province, China, after it was found.

Artifacts such as this bronze sword have helped archaeologists understand much about the lives of those who lived in ancient Greece.

The bronze mirror is an example of an artifact. Artifacts are objects made by humans. Natural objects are artifacts, too, if humans have changed them. Carved bones or knives made from stone are artifacts. Archaeologists study artifacts to learn about how ancient people lived. There are many mysteries about the past, and artifacts can help people piece together solutions to these mysteries.

Consider This

Archaeologists are scientists who learn about history by studying what people leave behind. What types of discoveries do you think archaeologists can use to help us learn about the past?

Treasure from Trash and Burials

There's an unexpected place where archaeologists often find artifacts: garbage pits. It might seem odd to dig in piles of old trash. However, garbage pits are good places to look if you want to learn about people who lived in the past. Garbage shows what people ate and how they lived. Archaeologists found scissors, thimbles, and needles in the garbage of a family who lived in the American colonies in the 1700s. Those artifacts showed that the family probably made most of their own clothes.

The discovery of artifacts can help guide the creation of replicas, such as this replica of a colonial home in Plymouth, Massachusetts.

This necklace was found among other jewelry in the tomb of Egyptian princess Sithathoryunet. It was found in Egypt in 1914.

Archaeologists also find artifacts in graves. Buttons and jewelry can last a long time in a grave. Some cultures buried personal belongings with their dead. Archaeologists also find **religious** artifacts and weapons in graves. These items can not only tell archaeologists about how a person lived, but also their position in society.

WORD WISE

RELIGIOUS MEANS RELATING TO RELIGION, WHICH IS A BELIEF IN AND WAY OF HONORING A GOD OR GODS.

Archaeologists uncover artifacts in many places beyond just ancient garbage pits and gravesites. Places where cities or buildings used to be are often full of artifacts. So are the ruins of churches and temples. After a very long time, buildings fall down. Over the years, dirt covers the ruins. Archaeologists sometimes have to dig through many layers of dirt to find artifacts.

The cave where ancient paintings were found in France in 1940 came to be called Lascaux Cave. The paintings offer clues about people's lives before written history!

In July 2022, archaeologists discovered a ritual bath that dates back to the first century CE near the Temple Mount in the ancient city of Jerusalem, Israel.

Sometimes people find artifacts by accident. A farmer might uncover an old grave while plowing a field. Someone digging a foundation for a building might discover remains of an older building on the same site. In France in 1940, four teenage boys followed a dog down into the entrance of a cavern. Inside they found a large cave with around 600 animals and **symbols** painted on its walls! Studies showed these paintings may date back to around 17,000 years ago.

WORD WISE

A SYMBOL IS A PICTURE, SHAPE, OR OBJECT THAT STANDS FOR SOMETHING ELSE.

Large and Small

Artifacts can range from large buildings to small objects you can hold in your hand. The pyramids are huge tombs for the royalty of ancient Egypt. The largest pyramid is 449 feet (137 meters) tall.

Ancient Egyptians believed they would live in another world after they died. They filled their tombs with things they would need there. Archaeologists have found food, clothing, and even board games in the pyramids. Paintings on the walls show scenes from everyday life. The pyramids and their contents help us learn about the lives of ancient Egyptians.

In 2023, studies of small objects found at a site in southern Oregon showed that it is the oldest place where humans have ever lived in North America! These items included a camel tooth and an orange tool made of a stone called agate.

The largest of Egypt's pyramids is the Great Pyramid of Giza, also called the Great Pyramid of Khufu. It originally stood about 482 feet (147 m) tall, but has shrunk over time due to erosion.

compare and contrast

How do you think what archaeologists can learn differs for small objects, like coins, versus large objects, like pyramids? And how do you think their findings are similar?

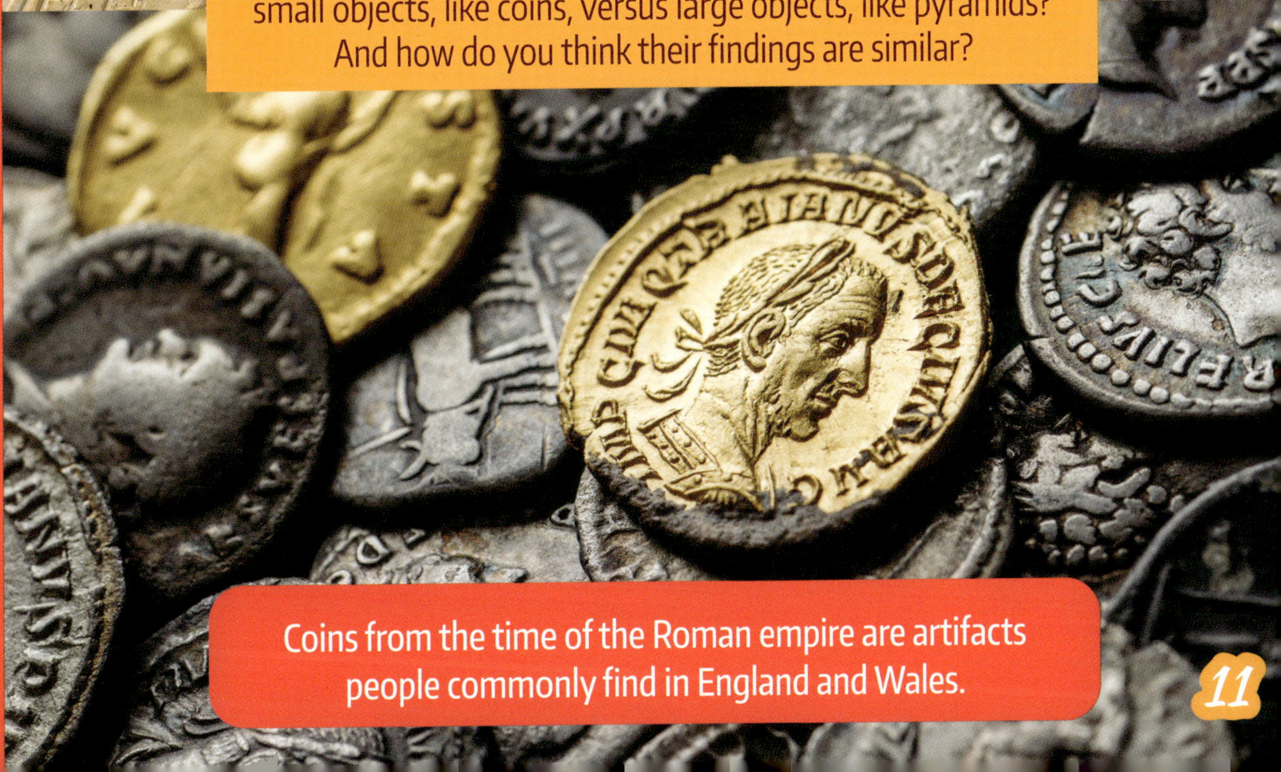

Coins from the time of the Roman empire are artifacts people commonly find in England and Wales.

Discoveries from the Past

Finding objects such as clothing, tools, or decorations that were used hundreds or even thousands of years ago can be thrilling! But artifacts are more than just objects that look cool. They help us to understand how people lived. Artifacts teach us about the daily lives of ordinary people. We learn what they ate, what they wore, and what kinds of games they played. We learn the type of work they did and which gods they worshipped.

Artifacts teach us what life was like during the historical periods we study. They help us understand the history we learn from books, documents, and letters. Artifacts also can give us information, or facts, not found in books or other writings. It is important to learn about people in the past. This can help people avoid mistakes made in the past, and it can help societies find better ways forward.

Special jars called canopic jars were used to store the organs of those who died in ancient Egypt. Organs are inside parts of a person's or animal's body.

compare and contrast

How do you think artifacts from modern times are similar and different from artifacts made hundreds or thousands of years ago?

In some African cultures, it's believed that a spirit makes its home in a mask after it is made. When someone wears the mask, it's believed the spirit can then take the person over.

Recent Artifacts

People often first think of items that are very old when they hear the word "artifact." People may think of Stonehenge, a Neolithic stone monument, that was built more than 3,000 years ago. Or they may picture the pyramids in Egypt that are more than 4,000 years old. Another example: Archaeologists found 10,000-year-old shoes in Oregon. A boat discovered in England is more than 3,000 years old. These artifacts are very old.

Kermit the Frog was first introduced on the show *Sam and Friends* in 1955. Kermit, along with other puppets such as Miss Piggy, became famous on the popular TV series *The Muppet Show*, which ran from 1976 to 1981.

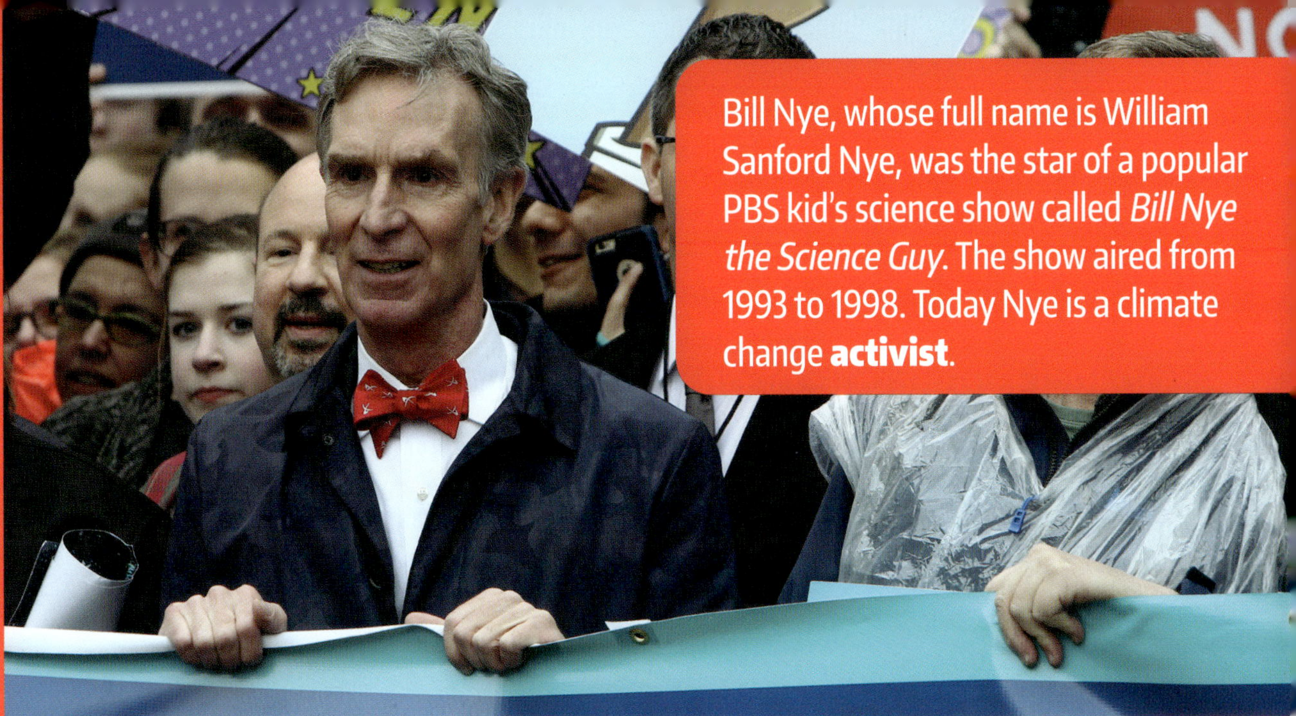

Bill Nye, whose full name is William Sanford Nye, was the star of a popular PBS kid's science show called *Bill Nye the Science Guy*. The show aired from 1993 to 1998. Today Nye is a climate change **activist**.

But artifacts don't have to be that old. The Henry Ford Museum in Dearborn, Michigan, has one of the first Apple computers. Steve Wozniak and Steve Jobs built it in 1976. The Smithsonian Museum holds the Simba mask from the musical *The Lion King* and the first Kermit the Frog Muppet. Bill Nye the Science Guy's lab coat is also in the Smithsonian. One archaeologist became famous for studying artifacts in the form of garbage people threw out in Tucson, Arizona, in the 1970s! There is much people can learn from recent artifacts.

WORD WISE

AN ACTIVIST IS A PERSON WHO USES OR SUPPORTS STRONG ACTIONS TO HELP MAKE CHANGES IN POLITICS OR SOCIETY.

How Old Is It?

It's important that archaeologists find out how old an artifact is. The age of an artifact tells them what period of history it belongs to. In some ways, archaeologists are like **detectives**. They examine artifacts for clues. There are many clues to the age of an artifact.

The rocks that make layers, almost like a birthday cake, that archaeologists can use to help tell the age of an artifact are called sedimentary rocks. The rock layers are called strata.

Scientists are discovering that the remains of human activities from 1950 until the present affect layers of rock. This shows how human activities have greatly affected Earth's land, water, and air.

Archaeologists often use more than one method to decide the age of an artifact. Sometimes they look at other objects found nearby. Those objects may tell them when the artifact was made or used. Archaeologists also can study the rock layers near the artifact. That scientific work is called stratigraphy. Soil and rock gradually build up in layers over the years. Scientists study when each layer was deposited. Studying the layers made by nature and shaped by different cultures can help archaeologists understand how the site was created and how it has changed over time.

WORD WISE

A DETECTIVE IS A PERSON WHO WORKS TO FIND INFORMATION ABOUT SOMEONE OR SOMETHING.

Studying nearby objects and the rock layers in which artifacts are found are not always the best ways to tell how old an artifact is. Sometimes archaeologists need a more dependable way to date artifacts. In those cases, they might use carbon dating.

Carbon dating can date the remains of people, animals, and plants. All living things have a substance called carbon-14. When they die, this substance slowly decays. Scientists measure the carbon-14 left in the remains of once-living matter. That amount tells them when the living thing died.

A professor at the University of Chicago named Willard Libby first proposed the idea of carbon dating in 1946.

Recent studies have shown that the burning of fossil fuels releases gases into the atmosphere that make carbon dating less effective.

Paper and wood have carbon because they are made from plants. Carbon dating was used to date the Dead Sea Scrolls, ancient texts found in the Middle East. Many artifacts do not have carbon, but they might have bits of organic material on them. For example, a sword might have traces of blood. By dating the blood, archaeologists can tell how old the sword is. Like other methods, carbon dating is not perfect. Some objects, specifically those that are older than 50,000 years, cannot be accurately dated.

Consider This

Artifacts younger than 100 years cannot be accurately carbon-dated because they have a very small amount of carbon-14. What are some other ways to determine the age of recent artifacts?

Training and Tools

A site is the term for a place where artifacts have been found. At a site, archaeologists do not just shovel piles of dirt. They are very careful. It takes many years of training to do their work properly. Before they start digging, they prepare the site. They divide the site into grids. That way, when they find something, they know exactly which part of the site it came from. They take photographs, or pictures, of the site. They also make lots of notes.

These archaeologists are working at a site in Macedonia that used to be an important ancient city in the Roman empire.

When archaeologists excavate a site, they carefully remove earth to find things that can tell them about the past, such as pots or bones. This takes patience, or the ability to wait.

Archaeologists do not usually use big shovels. They use small trowels and penknives. They do not want to miss small artifacts. Even if they discover something big, like a buried wall or building, they are very careful not to damage it. When working at a site, archaeologists need a lot of patience. It can take decades to finish preparing and **excavating** a site.

WORD WISE

EXCAVATING IS MOVING EARTH, ROCK, AND OTHER MATERIALS USING TOOLS.

Traditionally, archaeologists use their hands and simple tools to do most of their work. Today they have high-tech tools for finding and recovering artifacts. Satellite imagery programs like Google Earth can help archaeologists find remote sites. Drones can photograph sites from the air. X-rays make it possible to examine artifacts without disturbing them. Some archaeologists have used a robotic snake. The snake has explored caves dug by ancient Egyptians.

Drones are unmanned aircraft that are remotely controlled. They can be used to take photos of archaeological sites from the air.

Recent software has made ground-penetrating radar, shown at right, more effective. Software is a computer code, or program, that instructs a computer what to do.

Archaeologists collect a lot of data about sites and artifacts. Modern computer programs help to sort that data. Some computer programs make virtual representations of sites. Archaeologists use these representations to study the site. Virtual sites also can be used to teach people about archaeology. Ground-penetrating radar is another modern tool first used in the 1980s. It uses **radar pulses** to capture images below the ground's surface.

WORD WISE

RADAR IS A WAY OF USING RADIO WAVES TO FIND OBJECTS. A PULSE IS A QUICK INCREASE IN AN AMOUNT OF LIGHT, ELECTRICITY, OR SOUND.

Keeping Artifacts Safe

It is important that archaeologists take certain steps to keep the artifacts they find safe. Exposure to light and air can harm artifacts. A piece of cloth might last thousands of years in a dry tomb. However, it could quickly rot when exposed to damp air. Archaeologists look carefully at the conditions of the site where they find an artifact. Then they try to make as few changes as possible when they move it. Sometimes artifacts are treated with **chemicals** to help preserve them, or keep them safe.

Ways to preserve artifacts have changed a lot over the years. For example, one way to preserve the Sistine Chapel (shown on the right) during the 17th and 18th centuries was to use wine and sponges created from bread!

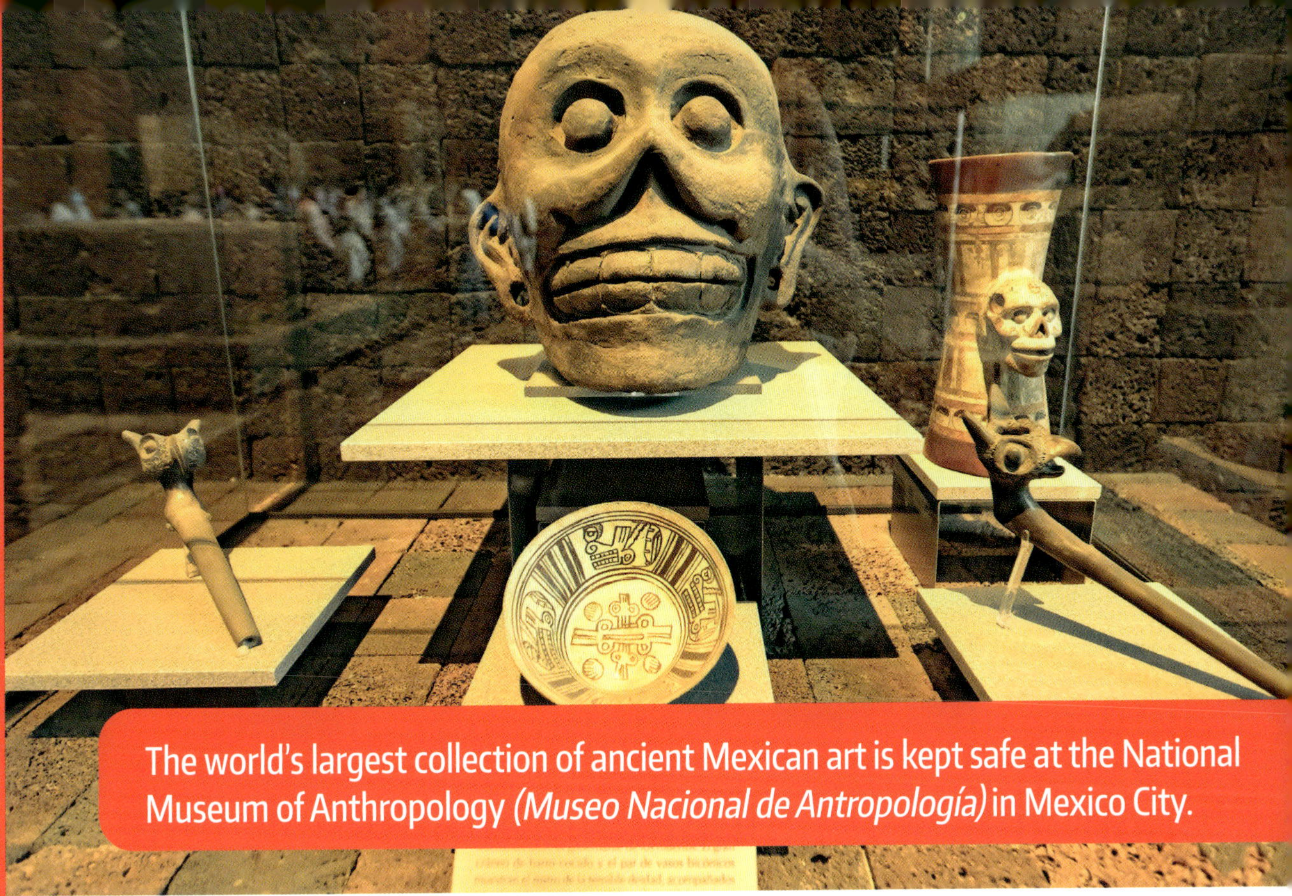

The world's largest collection of ancient Mexican art is kept safe at the National Museum of Anthropology *(Museo Nacional de Antropología)* in Mexico City.

After artifacts are collected, they usually are stored in museums. Museums have special rooms and cabinets for protecting artifacts. Museums may allow visitors to touch some artifacts. However, many artifacts are kept in cases to preserve them, and it is best to touch them as little as possible.

WORD WISE

A CHEMICAL IS MATTER THAT CAN BE MIXED WITH OTHER MATTER TO CAUSE CHANGES.

Lessons from the Past

People have created many different societies throughout human history. Those societies changed and sometimes collapsed. Past societies faced many of the same problems we do. They had wars and peace. They had times of plenty and times of famine. By studying artifacts, we learn how people in the past faced those problems. That knowledge can help us make better choices about our own future, or time to come.

Ancient monasteries in Assam, India, are built somewhat like the long houses shown in the above photo to withstand the flooding of the Brahmaputra River.

Climate change and its effects, such as rising seawater, are a danger to many artifacts, such as the Ruins of Kilwa Kisiwani in Tanzania.

Today we are experiencing climate change much faster than ever before. The climate has changed before. People in the past had to deal with ice ages, droughts, and floods. Artifacts show us how they managed. We can learn about the kinds of houses they built and the foods they grew when their climate was changing. Artifacts teach us how they built dams and stored rainwater. On the river island of Majuli in Assam, India, ancient monasteries are among those that have been built to withstand the Brahmaputra River's annual flooding.

Consider This

Many people are responding to climate change by using more renewable energy, or energy from sources that are naturally renewed, such as solar and wind. What do you think people in many years to come could learn from today's renewable energy machines they may discover as artifacts?

People Power

Studying artifacts can give people a clearer picture of what life was like for past societies. It helps us make better choices about the future. It also helps us in the present. Past cultures were very different from cultures today. But we can still find similarities between past ways of life and the ways people live now. Learning about past cultures can help us understand different cultures in our world today.

Cathedrals such as St. Stephen's Cathedral, shown here, are important churches led by bishops. They were first built during the Middle Ages and teach people today much about the religious practices of the past.

These artifacts can tell people about the life of the founder of the Hershey chocolate company, Milton Hershey, who was born in 1857.

Archaeologists work all over the world. They use many techniques and tools to find and preserve artifacts. They study human-made objects from the Stone Age to today. They study clothing and cathedrals, tools and temples, graveyards and garbage. Artifacts are objects that people made and used. However, archaeologists study artifacts not only to learn more about these interesting objects, but also to learn about the stories of the people who made and used them.

Consider This

What buildings or tools do you use today that could one day be considered artifacts? What do you think people in years to come could learn from them?

Glossary

bronze A type of metal made by combining copper and tin
collapse To suddenly fail, stop working, or completely break down.
culture The characteristic features of everyday life shared by people in a particular place or time.
data Information that is used in calculating, reasoning, or planning.
decay To lose strength; to break down.
deposit To lay down, place, or put.
document A written or printed paper containing information, usually legal or official information.
empire A large area of land under the control of a single ruler.
erosion The act of wearing away by water, wind, or ice.
exposure The state of being uncovered or unprotected.
famine An extreme shortage of food.
fossil fuel Matter formed over millions of years from plant and animal remains that is burned for power.
monastery A place where monks work and live. Monks are members of faith communities who often promise to stay poor, unmarried, and apart from society.
organic Having to do with living things.
ritual A formal ceremony.
thrill To cause someone to feel very happy or excited.
tomb A house or burial chamber for dead people.
trowel A small hand tool with a curved blade, often used by gardeners.
virtual Occurring or existing primarily online.

For More Information

Books

Hanel, Rachael. *An Ellis Island Time Capsule: Artifacts of the History of Immigration.* North Mankato, MN: Capstone Press, 2021.

Sheffield, Gary. *World War I Told Through 100 Artifacts.* New York, NY: Cavendish Square, 2019.

Thomas, Rachael L. *Uncovering Ancient Artifacts.* North Mankato, MN: Checkboard Library, 2019.

Websites

ArchaeOlogy: Clues from the Past
www.amnh.org/explore/ology/archaeology
Find fun games, videos, and more on this website from the American Museum of Natural History.

Artifacts
education.nationalgeographic.org/resource/artifacts/
Discover more information about how artifacts provide clues from the past here.

Britannica Kids: Artifact
kids.britannica.com/students/article/artifact/316586
Learn more about artifacts and their importance to archaeologists here.

Index